Sunday Worship

by
David Kennedy
Tutor in Liturgy, the Queen's College, Birmingham

and
David Mann
Member of Staff, St. George's Church, Leeds

 GROVE BOOKS LIMITED
Bramcote   Nottingham   NG9 3DS

CONTENTS

THE COVER PICTURE

is by Henry Martin

First Impression July 1989

ISSN 0144-1728

ISBN 1 85174 117 8

1. INTRODUCTION

Historically, Anglican Churches have stood in an inherited tradition of public worship on Sunday evenings. It seems obvious that in many areas where this still exists it is in decline and disarray, and we will suggest some reasons for this below. It is noteworthy that many of the new 'let's start from scratch' Independent Churches ('House churches' etc.) meet only once on Sundays, albeit for an extended meeting. While lay people might not feel guilty about attending worship only once, many clergy are troubled by the demise of their evening services. They may be tempted to ask the question, 'Does my church actually need a second service on a Sunday?'.[1] It is the conviction of this booklet that, given recent developments in Anglican morning worship, there is now more than ever a greater need to take the teaching, pastoral and evangelistic opportunities afforded by an evening service seriously. We suspect that in many parishes evening worship simply limps along. We want to suggest that such parishes think carefully about working out a yearly, or at least quarterly, programme and perhaps incorporate some of the ideas outlined below—not merely to cater for those who for whatever reason are disenfranchised from morning communion or family worship, nor for an alternative congregation, but that the church may be a better vehicle for mission, Christian nurture and the pastoral care of the whole Body of Christ. Much of what is written presupposes a church where an evening service already exists. We realize that this might not be the situation in some churches, particularly in the rural areas, but we hope the suggestions will none the less be of value in planning for special and incidental events.

---

[1] The last booklet in this series, *Worship in Small Congregations* by David Cutts will be helpful and relevant to many.

2. 'THIS IS THE DAY'

'Wherefore I pray and beseech you, as many as are here present, to accompany me with a pure heart, and humble voice, unto the throne of the heavenly grace . . .' *(Introduction to the General Confession, Evening Prayer, BCP).*

In many parishes today there would be a good case for substituting 'few' for 'many'. Sunday evening worship is not what it once was to the extent that some churches have abandoned it altogether while others have relegated it to a 12-seater side-chapel or struggle on with a sparse congregation spread thin throughout the barn of a building. Of course, there are exceptions and examples can be found of churches packing them in on a Sunday evening for liturgies both ancient and modern. But, as a trend across the country, it can scarcely be doubted that attendance at Sunday evening worship has been and is in serious numerical decline and that in terms of planning and expectation, it comes a very poor second to what happens in the morning.

The reasons for this general trend are not difficult to find and can be grouped under two headings.

1. The changing face of Sunday.

It is not too long ago that there would have been nothing unusual in hearing clergy preaching from pulpits that a proper honouring of the Lord's Day means, amongst other things, attending church both morning and evening. Sunday as the Christian Sabbath was, after the manner of the fourth commandment, to be kept holy and it was a matter of Christian responsibility to be present at the public worship of the church. However, over the last thirty years, the sabbatarian presuppositions of such a view have been increasingly challenged and Sunday has come to be regarded not so much as a day of rest but as a day for worship in celebration of Christ's resurrection. In society in general, Sunday is largely regarded as a day of leisure, and many Christians now regard the day as an opportunity for pursuing leisure interests. The result is that for many church members, the duty of witnessing to Christ's resurrection is fulfilled by a single attendance, normally in the morning. An example of the effect of secular influence upon the worship of the church is readily illustrated by the Roman Catholic Saturday evening vigil Mass which counts as Sunday duty (based partly on the Jewish reckoning of the day as extending from sunset to sunset); although this was originally authorized for the benefit of continental shift-workers it is now popular for the very reason that it allows an unencumbered Sunday for the pursuit of family and leisure interests.

2. Changing trends in worship.

Two factors are particularly relevant here. The first is the advent of the Parish Communion Movement which, from the 1920's, swept through

[1] For a discussion of the issues relating to the Christian understanding of Sunday, see W. Rordorf's magisterial work *Sunday: The History of the Day of Rest and Worship in the Earliest Centuries of the Christian Church,* (SCM Press, 1968).

the majority of Anglican parishes and has gained wide acceptance. The Movement is based on a central morning celebration of the eucharist and this service is to be the priority for all communicant Christians. Beginning as a Catholic Movement within the Church of England, any question of an evening communion service was ruled out because at that time evening celebrations of the eucharist were illegal in the Roman Catholic Church and in any case the rules on fasting demanded a reasonably early service. In receiving weekly communion, the Christian has fulfilled his or her duty and, while additional services may well be beneficial, they were not regarded as mandatory. In practice, the Movement underlined the trend towards a single attendance and greatly contributed to the trend; it also established the 'norm' of morning worship.

The second factor is the growth of 'family worship' within the Church of England. This trend originated in more evangelical parishes, and, like the Parish Communion Movement, has gained influence further afield. In many parishes, the attempt is to provide a genuine all-age form of service in which the entire church, from youngest to oldest, is mobilized and nurtured. Because of the sheer comprehensiveness of the idea, there is a strong sense that it is this act of worship that brings the whole church together so that other services again appear rather less than central to the life of the congregation.

Other factors can be added. The increasing insecurity of our nation means that many people are afraid to venture out after dark. Economic problems are posed for some parishes in keeping huge buildings warm for small evening congregations. It is not surprising, then, that evening worship is in crisis in many areas. However, we believe that parishes which allow Sunday evening worship to die almost by default or who give sparse thought or attention to what is on offer as an evening act of worship are missing a great opportunity. Much of this conviction arises from a concern that certain features of the Parish Communion or Family Worship pattern are not altogether helpful for the following reasons:

1. Constraints on time. A Parish Communion, for example, sets a Christian assembly a large agenda. Provision must be made for the ministry of the word, intercessions, ministry of the sacrament including the distribution perhaps to multiples of 100, hymnody, announcements. The ministry of the word can extend to three readings and a psalm with a sermon. There may be large numbers of children present demanding that the service be not as long as perhaps an exclusively adult congregation could stand. On top of this, there is still an unwritten law operating in many parishes that the whole thing should be over within the hour. What normally suffers is the sermon/teaching element. If additional elements are included such as baptisms or the ministry of healing, the limits are stretched to the extreme. Similarly, All-Age or Family Worship, by its very nature, is normally shorter rather than longer; most publications on the subject suggest anything from 40 minutes to an hour.

2. Popularization. Much morning worship now adopts what can be regarded as the 'tabloid approach' to Christian faith. Many Parish Communion sermons are short, snappy words of exhortation based around the Sunday theme and deliberately pitched for simplicity. Likewise, many Family Service addresses deal with Christian basics in a pictorial and dramatic fashion because they are aimed at fringe members of the congregation and have an eye towards children and teenagers. While some of this may be compensated for by other events such as home groups, the Sunday worshipping and teaching life of the church remains on a popular level unless parishes make a determined effort to the contrary. From our experience, many do not.

3. Lack of scope for creativity. This is a particular problem for the classic Parish Communion. While there is an argument that rhythm is important and a basic structure should be retained, it is a sad fact that the Alternative Service Book is still treated like The Book of Common Prayer, as if it set out to provide rigid and inflexible forms of service. But what happens in a parish with an inflexible Parish Communion and no evening worship? What provision can there be in the main assembly for other aspects of the array of possibilities open to a creative and visionary parish? Can there never be opportunity for special services, or an unhurried presentation by young people or children or an extended ministry of healing or forms of local indigenized liturgical worship?

4. A desire to worship. The fact remains that there are still many people who actually desire to worship and are prepared to give more than a minimum attendance, and look to their local Christian communities to give thought and prayer and consideration to this matter. In churches touched by charismatic renewal this is very noticable. Moreover, if morning worship is up-beat, noisy and activistic, there will be a need for a contrast. If the bulk of morning teaching is short and sharp for whatever reason, there will be a need for some provision of unhurried, digested, systematic teaching. The time is ripe for a new look at what our churches are actually providing. But before we look at possibilities for the future we will be wise to consider where we have come from.

3. 'ALL OUR YESTERDAYS'

'With the support of the Oxford Movement in the last century, the liturgical movement and now the charismatic movement in this century, the eucharist is now seen as the central weekly worship by many in all traditions of the Church. The future should see the abandonment of compromise monthly patterns giving choices of morning prayer, family service or communion on different Sundays and a return to a simplicity of eucharistic pattern that characterized the early church.' (Trevor Lloyd, *The Future of Anglican Worship*, Grove Worship Series 100, page 15).

Such a statement of eucharistic centrality would have been unthinkable in the Church of England 100 years ago. Apart from what was then a minority of parishes feeling the impact of second generation Tractarianism, the rank and file of clergy in the Church of England served up a diet of Mattins and Evensong for their Sunday congregations. This in itself had a long development from the Reformation. While it is clear from Cranmer's rubrics in the two Prayer Books of Edward VI that he intended a Sunday morning sequence of Mattins, Litany and Holy Communion with Evensong in the evening, the stubborn laity, used only to receiving the sacrament once a year at Easter, 'voted with their feet'. The intended communion became Ante-Communion with the minimalist instruction that the sacrament should be received at least three times a year including Easter Day. Moreover, in Cranmer's scheme of things, Sunday Mattins and Evensong were no different in essence from the weekday offices at which the laity were also expected to be present, but probably were not in any large numbers. This is made clear by the consecutive Scripture readings throughout the week.

It was the Oxford Movement that fundamentally challenged the prevailing non-sacramental *status quo*. Although an 8 a.m. weekly said communion became popular in Victorian times across the church, the classical Anglo-Catholic main morning service (occupying the then universal holy hour of 11 a.m.) was a High Mass, excelling in music and ceremonial but without a general communion of the people who would have been expected to have received, fasting, at an earlier 'low' celebration. But the Oxford Movement also had implications for how the offices were presented. This was especially true of Evensong, as Mattins in many parishes tended to become a Clergy devotion early in the morning before the first public service, and the influence of the Movement soon became normative in many parishes of a traditional Anglican ethos. One important element was the Cambridge Camden Society, which, in its periodical *The Ecclesiologist*, popularized a romantic approach to Church architecture based on the perceived glories of the medieval period, when chancels were filled with robed clergy and religious, singing to the glory of God. Such a vision led directly to the popularization of robed choirs, seated in longitudinal stalls, in newly built, extended or resurrected chancels. The renaissance of English choral music from the mid-Victorian period, along with the popularisation of the Anglican chant, saw the dawning of 'choral offices' as we know them today. With the introduction of regular hymnody following particularly the publication of *Hymns Ancient and Modern* in 1861, the service of Evensong, led by a choir with chanting, sung responses, hymns, an anthem and other ceremonial embellishments[1], meant that the service felt very different from the 'reading of prayers' (with perhaps an anthem or plain-chant by the singers in the westward gallery) of previous centuries. Of course, the development of the choral offices owed much to the example of the cathedrals following a general return to a greater care and dignity in worship that was a very welcome fruit of the later decades of the nineteenth century.[2] The reality was, however, that every parish church should become a little cathedral, and to be fair, there is a sociological perspective that is relevant here. In days of much greater church attendance and in an age pre-dating television, a typical parish church in town and country provided a much greater social framework than is the case today, with parish Institutes and the proliferation of organizations. Choral singing itself, one suspects, was far more popular as a pastime than now, and before about 1950, examples can be found of additional mid-week services of sung Evensong in populous parishes.

But it was the advent of the Parish Communion Movement that was to have the greatest impact on how the Sunday offices were perceived. The Movement, generally dated from the mid-1920s[3], was founded on the utter centrality of the eucharist for parish worship—'The Lord's service for the Lord's people on the Lord's Day', the form of worship the Church is commanded to observe. The Movement spread rapidly (though not in traditional evangelical parishes and more slowly in definite 'low church' but not necessarily evangelical churches). The important fact for our purposes is that the Movement set up a hierarchy of services. Attendance at the eucharist was non-negotiable; attendance at the offices was desirable but additional. This was fine as long as 'twicing' was fashionable, but with the incessant drift towards one attendance per Sunday for many, the Parish Communion lobby heralded loud and clear what was to be the priority. But there is another factor, arising from the church's increased eucharistic consciousness. Back in 1937, Henry de Candole wrote:

> 'Mattins and Evensong, the daily Offices of our Prayer Book, would deserve longer treatment than we can give. Much criticism is levelled against them, not a little of it due to a misconception of their object. They are not meant for beginners in the way of worship. They were never constructed as a substitute for the Eucharist. They are subsidiary services for the faithful communicant, satellites around the sun. To appreciate them demands considerable spiritual experience, *and they lack the dramatic action of the sacraments.*'[4]

[1] Such as turning eastwards for the Creed, bowing (or turning eastwards) at the *Gloria Patri*, extinguising the candles after the Third Collect, censing the Holy Table at the *Magnificat*.

[2] See, for example, the essay 'English Cathedral Music—A Glorious Habit' by Christopher Dearnley in (Ed) Robin Sheldon *In Spirit and in Truth*, (Hodder and Stoughton, 1989), pp. 121-122.

[3] For a recent discussion of the origins of the Movement, see Donald Gray, *Earth and Altar*, (Alcuin Club, Canterbury Press, 1986), part 3.

[4] From the essay 'Instruction in Worship' from (Ed) A.G. Hebert, *The Parish Communion*, (SPCK, 1937), p.241. (Italics ours).

8

The fact is that the Parish Communion provided a dramatic form of worship with movement, colour, ceremonial and the central action of getting out of the pew and going up to receive. Moreover, it was more participatory. In contrast, Evensong was static, cerebral, dominated by the choir with the almost impossible expectation that psalmody can be sung confidently and enjoyably from an unpointed Prayer Book.[1] The cry went up, 'I don't like evensong' in the face of clergy exhortations to attend as they saw the numbers falling.[2]

In general terms, evening worship is better supported in evangelical parishes, where the tradition of 'twicing' is stronger, although there has been a trend towards a single attendance. Evangelical parishes have tended to resist the introduction of a Parish Communion, despite the resolution at the 1967 Keele Congress that the Holy Communion should be the central act of worship on Sunday. Monthly patterns still persist and there has also been a tradition of a rather free-er approach to statutory services and a greater emphasis on preaching.

As the Church of England begins to look towards the next round of liturgical revision, it appears that non-sacramental worship is beginning to receive more attention. The ASB was a conservative revision in this respect but the shorter forms of Morning and Evening Prayer have been welcomed for both weekday and Sunday worship. Writers such as George Guiver are making a plea for a far more wholesale revision of the Office for the future.[3] The Liturgical Commission is at present working on material for 'Services of the Word' with special coaching on how to put such acts of worship together. It may well be that over the next few years there will be a greater variety of options than ever before. In the suggestions that follow below, a parish would have to call upon a whole variety of resources. Whether it opts for a service based on the Office or the kind of DIY material being worked on by the Commission, it is to be hoped that a degree of flexibility will be provided to serve the needs of the infinite variety of possibilities to which the church should respond.

---

[1] While it is true that robed choirs, processions, gestures, etc., did give some drama and ceremonial to Evensong this is slight in comparison to what was happening at the Parish Communion. Moreover, Evensong lacked a sense of climax in places where expectations of the sermon were low.

[2] It should be stated that Choral Evensong can be and is a growth service in some parishes, especially where there is a competent choir. As well as careful choice of music, creative intercessory material and, of course, a good sermon, will result in a satisfying act of worship.

[3] See his *Company of Voices: Daily Prayer and the People of God*, (SPCK, 1988), parts III & IV.

4. IDEAS AND PATTERNS FOR SUNDAY EVENING WORSHIP

1. Sunday Evening and Teaching

At least three factors have contributed to the demise of a comprehensive teaching element in Anglican Sunday worship: (i) the pressure of time in the parish communion which puts the squeeze on the Ministry of the Word, (ii) a 'lowest common denominator' approach to teaching in Family Worship, and (iii) the thematic approach in the present eucharistic lectionary. Despite efforts to hide the Sunday themes away on page 1092 of the ASB, the thematic approach now so dominates that we suspect sermons are preached on the theme without a careful getting to grips with the Scriptural passages. Likewise, liturgical resources such as contemporary hymnbooks with lists of hymns suggested for each Sunday, emphasize the theme rather than the readings. The list of themes and Biblical passages is necessarily selective and cannot hope to cover all aspects of Christian faith and living, or even give space for all the best stories. How is it possible to treat great themes in any depth? An evening service, it might be thought, could provide for greater variety of teaching. Even here, however, the lectionary presents a problem—the set readings for Evening Prayer are based on the same themes as the eucharist and in many cases eucharistic readings for year one appear as readings in year two Evening Prayer (and *vice versa*).[1] We hope that a wider choice of readings will be a feature of future lectionary revision. Colin Buchanan in his *Patterns of Sunday Worship* (Grove Ministry and Worship Booklet no. 9) suggests that emphasizing a teaching element in evening worship is the key to providing for the needs of, and holding onto, the rather heterogeneous group that comprises Sunday evening churchgoers.

a. Worship and the Sermon. That being the case, we wish it could be said that in the parishes that use Evensong it has been the quality of the preaching that has attracted people in the past. If that were so, then the simple advice to 'beef up' the sermon with teaching would be a sure crowd-puller. But it is not as straightforward as that. As much attention has to be paid to the other aspects of the service—the quality of the hymns and prayers. The preacher may be concerned lest the sermon be uninspiring—most of the congregation will be more upset if the hymns are drab and uninspiring, because hymnody is the element of the service in which they feel most involved. Provision is made in the ASB for the sermon to be preached after the second reading. On the whole, this produces a neat and balanced progression of praise-Scripture-prayer(response). However, one of the weakest links in this progression seems to be the movement from praise to Scripture. Most assume that this occurs after the singing of the psalm. But it would be better to think of the psalm as part of the Scripture section of the service and if it is to provide an adequate link (as it sometimes does) between praise and Scripture it must have some preceding praise to link into! As well as the canticle provided, this section needs at least a hymn (or a few choruses) to effect the

[1] For a further discussion of the role of the lectionary see Michael Vasey, *Reading the Bible at the Eucharist* (Grove Worship Series no. 94, 1986).

balance—and the psalm can then be treated more imaginatively.[1] To assume that any chanted psalm (for example, 'By the waters of Babylon ... ') does justice to the invitation, 'Let us worship the Lord', is laughable.[2]

b. Discussion and the Sermon. Preached at the end of the service, the sermon can lead on to discussion or feed-back afterwards over coffee. Many churches adopt this format during Lent and encourage people to attend and contribute as part of a Lenten discipline. But a series on particular pastoral needs (e.g. 'Coping with ... old age/adolescents/marital problems' etc.) will lend itself to this kind of treatment as well, and at any time of the year. Professionals from within the community (doctors, social workers, community nurses etc.) may feel it inappropriate to be invited to preach, but will gladly contribute to a seminar following a service. Some preachers risk feed-back even when the sermon follows the second lesson. This is perhaps best achieved by first facilitating discussion amongst the congregation (with specific questions to answer) and then a short plenary before prayers. This approach needs careful, if daring, nurture.

c. The Sermon Series. A number of churches use Evening Prayer as the platform for an extended teaching series, with a number of weeks devoted to the exposition of a book of the Bible, particular doctrines, Scriptural themes or social issues. Where attendance is in decline the introduction of a weighty teaching series needs careful preparation and publicity— sermon outlines available before the service, guest speakers invited (for their preaching ability as opposed to their ecclesiastical rank!) and, perhaps, co-ordinated study material (in advance) for a mid-week discussion group. [3] The reputation of the first of such a series will determine the success of subsequent attempts.

d. Alternatives to the traditional sermon. Colin Buchanan[4] suggests further alternative approaches to the sermon:

1. Lecture and questions : a 30-minute lecture followed by questions and further discussion over coffee.
2. Debate: an issue of faith or ethics approached from two perspectives with questions and an impartial 'referee' to sum up.
3. Conference: an introductory address followed by work in small groups coming together for a plenary with further questions and discussion.
4. Policy meeting: some aspect of parish life brought before the congregation for consideration and to increase awareness.
5. House groups: the possibility of dispersed meetings in homes.

At St. George's Leeds, the church 'shuts shop' on at least four Sunday evenings a year and three or four housegroups combine to meet for 'Area

[1] e.g. read out antiphonally; a responsorial or metrical version employed instead of/as well as; a dramatized version declaimed. For a range of musical possibilities, see (eds) Robin Leaver, David Mann and David Parkes, *Ways of Singing the Psalms*, (Collins, 1987).
[2] A hymn after the psalm also destroys this progression.
[3] Cf. C.P.A.S. 'Open House' integrated housegroup/sermon material.
[4] *Op. cit.* pp.16-18.

Worship' in different localities all over the city. They use mid-week meetings to construct their worship around a given theme, and can decide their own approach to a 'teaching slot'. A variety of styles has developed ranging from shared sermons, developed and delivered by a small group, through to Bible study input with space for testimony-style response from individuals who would like to contribute and then small group reflection. These small meetings provide a 'safe' environment in which to exercise a number of gifts in worship; it helps some individuals to gain confidence in talking about their faith, and others to try out a preaching or teaching ministry. Clarry Hendrickse[1] provides another example of this:

> 'On Sunday evenings we have four housegroups at 6.30 p.m. one of which is in the church lounge. People are allocated to these geographically. They discuss the morning teaching using guidance questions provided by the preacher. Lay Leaders run these. Every fourth Sunday there is a 'Come Together' holy communion in the Church which each housegroup will organise and lead in turn. A minister will preside and may be asked to preach.'[2]

e. Postscript. It may be that parishes will have to ask themselves whether Sunday evening is not a better time on which to hold church meetings. In places where commuting is common, virtually nothing can start on mid-week evenings until after 8 p.m.—and then it is a case of bringing sandwiches to house groups or P.C.C. meetings because there is no time to go home for a meal. As Friday and Saturday nights are increasingly times for leisure pursuits, it may be that Sunday evening is a good time for church groups to meet. Certainly a meeting starting at the traditional time of 6 or 6.30 will finish at a reasonably early hour compared with midweek meetings starting at 8 p.m.

Of course, in all of this, there may have to be a degree of selectivity where evening worship is in low water. But a lively set of meetings, say in Lent, could be a spring-board for further growth at other times of the year.

2. Evening Worship and Young People

In recent years we have seen a tendency towards the ideal of 'All-Age Worship'. This title is to some extent in reaction to 'Family Worship' on the basis that the presuppositions behind the word 'family' can suggest the marginalization of the single, widowed, divorced, etc.[3] Yet it is genuinely very difficult to cater adequately for all ages in a single service and there remains the suspicion that, despite the best intentions, the focus of attention falls on the adults and young children and the neglected group are the teenagers. Back in 1976, Michael Botting wrote:

> '12 or 13 plus: At this age the youngsters are beginning to flex their muscles of independence from the family, not in a spirit of rebellion

---

[1] *One Inner Urban Church and Lay Ministry,* (Grove Pastoral Series 13, p.17.

[2] Some churches build up a resource library of video and taped material from TV and radio to use as input at such housegroup sessions. These are usually broadcast around Lent for ecumenical discussion groups (note also the excellent 1989 BBC documentary series, with accompanying booklet, on Churches from different continents, *The Sword and the Spirit)* but can be used effectively integrated and spread out over the year.

[3] *Church Family* is the preferred solution by CPAS and Jubilate Hymns in their resource book *Church Family Worship.* The question of name is discussed in the supplementary publication *Church Family Worship Resource Book,* (CPAS, 1986,) pp.1-5.

necessarily, but in the natural processes of growing up and out. It would be a mistake to try to force teenagers to come with their parents to Family Service every week . . . It is better to allow the teaching of this group to continue as a separate part of the Church programme.'[1]

While this was written some time ago with a particular model in mind, it does acknowledge the difficulty. Many teenagers feel strongly that 'action-choruses' and addresses with activities or content related to children are exceedingly childish and not 'grown up'. Yet these same teenagers will often have acquired very real skills in contributing to worship as children and it would be foolish in the extreme for the church not to build upon this. Some strategy for teenagers to help with the planning and leadership of worship in which they can make their distinctive contribution, often employing gifts in drama, dance and music, is highly desirable. The popularity and training potential of Roman Catholic 'Folk Masses', often held on late Sunday afternoon or evening is something that the Church of England could well learn from. While such involvement need not necessarily be limited to evening worship, it seems likely that, given the programme of most parishes, this is the obvious place to start. Moreover, the popularity of Sunday evening youth groups means that there is in many places a ready constituency on which to build.[2]

3. Evening Baptisms
In his book *Believing in Baptism,* Gordon Kuhrt, writes on Canon B21:

'. . . baptism should normally be at a main Sunday Service (B21). This enables the new members to be welcomed properly into the Christian family, and for the whole congregation to be reminded of the sacrament and its rich significance for them all. Practical problems should not be allowed to lead to a regular ignoring of this Canon which has such clear and obvious theological justification. Rather, any practical problems should lead to a critical reconsideration of the parochial practice of worship, initiation, evangelism and nurture of young people in the Christian faith'.[3]

It is evident that such 'practical problems' relate primarily to morning worship. A regular administration of the baptism of children at a main act of Sunday morning worship can prove to be difficult because of a) sheer lack of space in the church building to accommodate the normal congregation and large baptismal parties; b) concern that the regular patterns of worship and preaching will be too often disrupted because the needs of the baptismal parties are deemed to be paramount; c) a service held early in the morning (9 a.m.—10 a.m.) creates problems for relatives and friends travelling from afar or presents the difficulty of organizing an infant and possibly other children for an early start.

[1] Michael Botting and John Tigwell, *Reaching the Families,* (Falcon, 1976), p.32.
[2] In Kenya, a united youth service called a 'rally' provides regular opportunity for training, cross-fertilization of ideas, publicity of youth-related events and contact with the diocesan youth advisor/chaplain. In Britain, some churches have used an evening service to host a 'Youth Quake' Christian rock-concert (incorporating contemporary music, drama, poetry, etc.) within the context of a simple act of worship with a low-key evangelistic thrust.
[3] See p.144.

Such practical difficulties often mean that the minister will settle for an afternoon 'hole in the corner' privatized service. One of us, having attended such a gathering recently at which five children were baptized in a 'said' service in the middle of the afternoon, found it instructive to talk with members of the family about what they made of it. A number commented that 'it didn't feel like a service'; it was more of a spectator event against a background of general chattering; there was little attempt and, it must be admitted, little in the ASB to encourage active participation by the 150-strong congregation.

The setting of baptism in a simple adapted evening service not only fulfils the intention of the canonical requirement but also provides a worshipping framework, which with sensitive and creative leadership and pastoral awareness of the church family can draw those on the fringe into an encounter with the risen Christ. It can also make the baptism feel much more of an event than the lifeless atmosphere of a private rite. This in itself relieves pressure on the morning service and provides a genuine mission opportunity. From experience, such an arrangement has proved popular with many families and a service as late as 6 p.m. has provided no greater difficulty than one before 10 a.m. Parishes wishing to adopt such a procedure may have to suggest some gentle coaching about time-table. It makes sense for the baptism tea to take place before the service; in places where social convention demands a visit to the pub, this naturally takes place after the service! If ASB Evening Prayer provides the frame-work, metrical versions of psalms and canticles make sense for those quite unable to cope with the Anglican chant!

4. Memorial and Anniversary Services

a. *The Bereaved.* In certain parts of England, for example, the North East and the Black Country, the tradition of mourners attending an evening service at some point after the death of a loved one is quite strong. The tradition is an old one, originating at a time when in many parishes, the evening service was the main service of the day in terms of attendance. Pastorally, the special atmosphere of evening worship is more helpful than the hustle and bustle of the morning, while many standard evening hymns speak directly of the reality of death.[1] The fact that the tradition survives even in urban areas where the vast majority of funerals take place at the cemetery or crematorium suggests that it meets a pastoral need, and we would suggest that even in areas where there is no such tradition, a local church might well consider suggesting the possibility to mourners as part of the church's ministry to them. It is certainly true that for many mourners, the trauma of the funeral is such that they 'hear' little of what is said and that they are much more likely to be receptive to a message of Christian hope at a later date. Moreover, the associations that a parish church has with events other than death can be genuinely helpful.

While in some cases no special provision is made for the mourners apart from the prayers of intercession, some parishes and especially those responsible for many funerals in the course of a month provide a 'memorial' or 'bereavement' service on a regular basis in the evening. Here, the needs of the mourners are paramount in the message of the sermon, the prayers and the careful choice of hymnody. This provides the

[1] For example, 'O Strength and Stay'; 'Glory to Thee, my God, This Night'; 'Sun of my Soul'; 'God that Madest Earth and Heaven'; 'Abide with me' etc.

opportunity for a sensitive proclamation of Christian hope and enables the congregation to show solidarity with the bereaved. If Evening Prayer is the form of service to be used (although some parishes will prefer a eucharist) careful adaptation will help participation and no effort should be spared in helping those unused to liturgical worship to feel part of what is happening.

b. Those to be married/the newly married. For churches conducting a number of weddings each year, the evening service can provide an excellent opportunity for teaching on Christian marriage. With the year's 'marriage diary' in mind, invitations would go out to those newly married (if still resident in the area) as well as those soon to be married. A combination of suitable drama (e.g. a mock 'Mr. & Mrs.'), honest testimony from established Christian couples, prayer for the strengthening of marriage, and Biblical teaching, perhaps leading on to discussion after the service over coffee, would not only supplement any marriage preparation classes but provide the church with an opportunity to reflect on Christian marriage and to invite others to do so.

5. 'Special' Sundays

'... unless the Church of England wishes to follow the way of a sect, it must be constantly on the look-out for occasions of ministering to its whole parish, and that must include the institutions in it and the places where its people work.' (Michael Perham, *Liturgy Pastoral and Parochial p. 217).*

Our generation has seen the proliferation of specially designated Sundays such as 'Hospital Sunday', 'Education Sunday', 'Sea Sunday', 'Industry Sunday' in addition to traditional observances such as Rogationtide. They seek to make connections between life and work or wider society. When added to other specials of a more churchly nature such as 'Missionary Sunday', 'Suffering Church Sunday', 'Tear Fund Sunday' etc., there may be a case of chronic over-load! However, in planning an annual number of 'special' Sundays, a creative church will want to look at the place in which it ministers and may wish to make provision for an invitation service based on the school or the hospital or the factory as a means of showing the Christian community's interest in its locality and the places where its people work or through which they are served. It also gives an opportunity to give a Christian perspective and to explore the relationship between faith and daily work. Because any institution or work-place will employ Christians of differing denominational loyalties this kind of initiative can profitably be undertaken ecumenically. In one semi-rural parish, invitations were sent out to the staffs of the ten farms within the parish boundaries advertising a special Rogationtide evening service. Representatives from six of the farms actually attended as well as other people employed on a casual basis and the reaction to the service (in which issues could be addressed far more seriously than the more popular Harvest Thanksgiving equivalent) was favourable. At the very least it showed that local Christians were interested and better pastoral links were nurtured. The contribution of local Christians working in the various fields of industry and commerce to the planning and leadership of such services is in itself a great opportunity for the furtherance of understanding and mission.

6. Creative Use of the Festivals

It seems a pity that many Christians' corporate celebration of the Resurrection should be limited to an hour or to an hour and a half on Easter Sunday morning. It is even sadder to turn up ' on spec' at a church on Easter Sunday evening, perhaps while on holiday, full of the joy of the Resurrection to find a damp squib of an Evensong with a dozen in the congregation straining for the top F of a paschal alleluia! If a Church settles for a low-key approach it will achieve a low-key response. If it genuinely encourages celebration, celebration there will be.

If 'twicing' as a general rule of life has indeed died, surely there is scope for a little bit of coercion at Festivals; indeed, many will want to celebrate. Most churches still give special emphasis to at least three of the following:

Christmas; Easter; Pentecost; Feast of Dedication/Patronal Festival; Harvest Thanksgiving.

Leaving aside Christmas for obvious reasons, we would suggest a two-fold pattern for a Festival Sunday:

PARISH COMMUNION— PRAISE SERVICE

Festival parish Communions bring their own special difficulties. For example, larger numbers of communicants can lead to greater stress on time generally while the presence of large numbers of fringe worshippers can have a limiting effect on the worship in any case. A second service gives more scope for a satisfying celebration and a form of worship more suited to creativity, employing such elements as drama, mime, dance, special music. Moreover, there will be more space for teaching than in a typical communion service. If, as is common, church buildings are beautifully and worshipfully decorated for festival Sundays, it seems a pity if such a setting is not enjoyed to the full. Churches need to learn to be extravagant in their celebration of the principal holy days.

7. Other Possibilities)

In some senses, this section is potentially limitless, but the following eight areas are particularly relevant.

1. Inviting the Bishop. This may be for such episcopal services as confirmation (although parish communion churches may well desire a morning service) or simply because it is desirable that bishops and congregations should get to know each other. Indeed, the sheer popularity of morning confirmations probably means that an evening service is the best way of getting hold of a bishop. Historically, the office of bishop has included an important teaching role[1] and again, it is likely that an evening act of worship would give space for something substantial as well as freedom from morning time restraints (Sunday lunch and all that) for informal fellowship afterwards.

[1] See, for example, Colin Buchanan's 'The Bishop in Action in (ed) Colin Buchanan, *The Bishop in Liturgy* (Alcuin/GROW Liturgical Study no. 6, 1988).

2. Guest/Evangelistic Services. Not many churches would choose a parish communion for such a purpose. Most successful evangelistic services are home-grown with a carefully thought out liturgy appropriate to those who have been invited along to hear the gospel. Sunday evening has always been the traditional time for such services and, as a special act of outreach, they should receive the active support and backing of the worshipping community if evangelism is central to the life of the church. A way of introducing such a service into a church's programme is to change the liturgical emphasis of an evening confirmation service. One model for this is if the service is billed as an 'Act of Witness with Confirmation'. Candidates provide testimonies for a service hand-out and two or three share brief testimonies within the context of the service. The bishop is asked to preach an evangelistic address, and there is an opportunity for those who would like to discover more about the Christian life to make a response at the end of the service.

3. Charismatic/Informal Worship. Many churches touched by charismatic renewal will operate a more traditional service in the morning and a more informal service at night. The latter gives space for the exercise of spiritual gifts in a way simply not possible at the earlier service because it is consciously 'all-age' with children and fringe members present or because it is felt necessary to retain a 'liturgical' or more traditional act of worship through which people will grow into a deeper experience of renewal. Generally speaking, charismatic Anglican churches do not have so much difficulty sustaining two main services because of the deep desire to worship evident among their adherents.

4. A Special Summer Programme. A possible programme for the summer season, or month of August, might involve balancing a short family worship/communion (with a 'beach mission' feel to it) in the mornings with a series of sermons in the evening: selected insights into the life of a Biblical character presented in all-age 'tabloid' activities in the mornings ('Desperate Dan!'; 'Holy Moses!' etc. with appropriate taped music and young peoples' songs) can be followed by more in-depth exposition of the passage, in parallel, in the evenings. This could key in with a young peoples' holiday club throughout the week.

Many churches in holiday resorts balance a formal morning service with an evening Songs of Praise. In limited doses this provides a welcome change to any parish's programme. The order follows a simple all-age hymn-sandwich of pre-requested, well-known favourites (chosen by different sections of the church and related organizations) and might include a short homily related to a particular hymn or its author(ess). With good planning and publicity, members of the local community could be invited to this service, and their choice of hymns be represented—but be aware that advertisements connecting the service to the TV series can be misleading!

5. Healing Services. John Richards, in his excellent book *The Question of Healing Services* provides a persuasive rationale for their place in the life of the church. Again, some parishes will want the ministry of healing to be

administered within the parish communion but there may well be com-
pelling reasons, whether ecumenical or practical, for a non-eucharistic
ministry and so an evening slot becomes a possibility.[1]

6. Ecumenical Worship. Traditionally, many Free Churches have maintained a strong evening service and for this reason Sunday evening may
commend itself for united worship. Certainly, if sacramental divisions are
to the fore, a non-sacramental service is probably the most helpful means
of Christians from diverse traditions learning to love and understand each
other. In reality, many ecumenical services become as much of a rump as
the evening services in the constituent denominations and careful
thought is needed if this sorry state of affairs is to be avoided.

7. Deanery/Diocesan Services. If Deaneries and Dioceses are to grow in a
sense of common purpose and unity, should there not be opportunities to
share worship together? A situation in which local churches meet
separately in the morning and then periodically come together in the evening for a united service seems to us to have great potential for strengthening bonds in what can be diverse areas. For smaller and even larger
congregations, the sense of belonging to something far greater is a source
of encouragement. With some adventurous pre-planning, choirs from the
locality (or even the Cathedral Choir) could be asked to contribute. The
bishops could also have a role here as teachers or such a setting could be a
creative way to deal with policy decisions.

8. An Evening of Prayer and Meditation. This form of evening worship
might precede some particular important decision to be made by the
church, or respond to a need for space to meditate during a period of particular activity—during the Christmas festivities for example. If the service
is to be devotional it should be reflected in the restrained choice of hymnody and in a simplicity of style. The service could be structured around
periods of prolonged silence and a theme maintained by Biblical (and
perhaps secular) readings. If a period of open/extempore prayer is unsuit-
able, a simple home-spun litany or the ASB litany could be used.[2] Intercessory prayer could be interspersed with a Taize responsorial chant or
round. Alternatively, the service could be modelled on a 'lucernarium' as
provided in the Order of Worship for the Evening (1979 American BCP), a
simple service marking the progression from day to night with meditation
around the lighting of candles and the singing of the 'Phos hilaron'('Hail
gladdening light'). Another way would be to conclude a time of meditation
and prayer with a modern form of Compline.[3]

This section has covered many ideas and they are offered as ideas, not in
any sense as a blueprint. To reiterate the point we made earlier, our plea is
that local churches should give careful thought to what they are doing in
their patterns of worship in order to see what opportunities are available,
and to ask whether Sunday evening can be used, albeit in a selective way, to
assist the on-going pastoral, evangelistic and teaching ministry of the church.

[1] John Richards sets out the relevant issues in chapters 8 -10.
[2] Cf. *The Worshipbook,* (Westminster Press, Philadelphia, 1970) for some excellent
litanies.
[3] Cf. Mark Davies *A Late-Night Service: Compline in Modern English* (Worship Series no.
72). There is also now a semi-official order of the Church of England.

5. PASTORAL AND PLANNING CONSIDERATIONS

Any endeavour to 'spice up' Sunday evening worship or to take on board the suggestions outlined above will demand time and investment in careful planning. Good ideas are cheap—but a vision for revitalising a parish's evening worship is costly. To begin with, a careful and realistic appraisal must be made of the particular pastoral problems that might occur. Congregations with fairly established and fixed patterns of worship may resent what they see as the incessant 'tinkering' with traditional Evensong, and feel that the needs of others are taking priority over their own needs—that they have lost 'their' service to 'others'. If the staff of a church fails to appreciate the subtle difference between the (fairly 'anonymous') leading of evening prayer as opposed to the (more 'up-front') management of some of the events outlined above, they may fall into the trap of presiding over a one-(wo)man floor show. Their personal ability to carry this off may also provoke resentments.

What is involved is an awareness that experimentation in worship patterns is profoundly threatening to staff and congregations alike—the ordained may remember the audible sigh of relief when a term of experimental worship in theological college came to an end(!)—and with it a totally different style of planning and ordering the worship. If the vision is to be perceived as owned by the whole of the congregation rather than imposed 'from above', a 'worship team' including both staff and lay-folk will need to spend much time understanding the objectives of such a revised attitude to evening worship as well as planning and being involved in it.

To begin with, careful thought needs to go into the membership of such a worship team. A group might naturally spring from the PCC, as a sub-committee, but needs to be inclusive of interested parties (the musicians!) and balanced (old and young). It needs to be representative of the parish, and not just a group of the Vicar's 'yes (wo)men' without being too large. If it is too small its views will be perceived as sectarian; if too many viewpoints are represented it will never get to the job in hand. People with special expertise can always be invited, at a later date, to contribute fresh insights—someone with skills in visual aids, a local drama teacher, etc. Subsequently, existing networks within the congregation can be motivated and involved—the Mothers' Union or Young Mums group set the project of designing a banner or flower-arrangements for a particular theme or sermon series. If established house-groups exist, particular events could be delegated to them. But all of this should only begin once the initial worship group has been set up and has had time to develop an atmosphere of mutual trust in which lay-folk can feel free to contribute (and reflect on successes and failures) and the staff have had time to cope with the ensuing enthusiasm (and resist the desire to haul in the reins if things do not go according to plan).

Preliminary meetings should be given over to discussion of the different individual likes and dislikes, expectations, and understandings of worship represented within the group. If the church is to come to terms with more adventurous and experimental patterns of evening worship, this group must themselves first undergo the process of coming to a common mind, devising and participating in such worship—culminating in producing a simple act of worship for themselves from scratch, using it 'from cold' on a mid-week evening in church and reflecting afterwards on the feelings that it aroused. The process will be an education in itself.

With this in hand, discussion of the wider evangelistic and pastoral potential for evening worship can begin. It is important that the congregation is not left in the dark as to what is happening and should at least feel part of the discussion at this point. A report to the PCC should be made available to the congregation and supported by verbal notices asking for prayer support.

The way is then clear for the worship group to analyze the liturgical calendar, decide on how much to tackle (a quarterly programme of evening events or a series spaced out equally over the year) and gain the PCC's support for a limited period of experimentation. For the events to make an adequate impact upon the worshipping life of the congregation this period should proceed in spite of hiccups; for adequate feedback from the church and positive reflection, a day of workshops on evening worship could be planned for the end of the experiment. The diocesan liturgical representative or liturgical group, if given enough warning (and if up to it!), could be asked to help facilitate such a day. Some churches provide the congregation with a questionnaire to provide comment on how they perceive what has been undertaken. This can prove very tricky to construct and even harder to analyze. Questionnaires tend to polarize opinions; a day workshop can focus rather on what has been helpful about the experiment, provide impetus for a way forward, and continue to raise on to the agenda of the church the need to take seriously the opportunities provided by an evening act of worship.